Raising a Family

Paul Bennett

Wayland

Nature's Secrets

Catching a Meal
Changing Shape
Communicating
Escaping from Enemies
Hibernation
Keeping Clean
Making a Nest
Migration
Pollinating a Flower
Raising a Family

Cover: A cheetah mother with her cubs in Kenya, Africa.
Title page: The female scorpion is a good mother. She carries her babies on her back to keep them safe.
Contents page: An adult spotted dolphin with its baby. Young dolphins are cared for by their parents for years.

Series editor: Francesca Motisi
Editor: Joan Walters
Series designer: Joyce Chester
Consultant: Stephen Savage
Stephen Savage provided the notes for parents and teachers.

First published in 1995 by
Wayland (Publishers) Ltd
61 Western Road, Hove
East Sussex BN3 1JD, England

© Copyright 1995 Wayland (Publishers) Limited

British Library Cataloguing in Publication Data

Bennett, Paul
Raising a Family – (Nature's Secrets Series)
I. Title II. Series
591.56

ISBN 0-7502-1554-2

Printed and bound in Italy by
G.Canale & C.S.p.A., Turin

Picture acknowledgements
The publishers would like to thank the following for allowing their photographs to be reproduced in this book: Bruce Coleman Ltd *title page* (Alan Stillwell), 5 (top/Konrad Wothe), 6, 10, 11/top and centre (Kim Taylor), 11/bottom, 12/bottom, 13 (Jane Burton), 18 (bottom/Jen and Des Bartlett), 19 (top/Austin James Stevens), 23 (bottom/S. Nielson), 24 (Werner Layer), 25 (top/M. R. Phicton); Natural History Photographic Agency *contents page*, 18/top (Kelvin Aitken), 4/top, 9 (John Shaw), 7 (both/Stephen Dalton), 8/bottom, 28/top (Anthony Bannister), 21 (Brian Hawkes), 23 (top/A.N.T.), 25 (bottom/Martin Harvey), 26 (Stephen Krasemann), 27 (top/David Woodfall), 27 (bottom/Nigel J. Dennis); Oxford Scientific Films *cover* (Daniel J. Cox), 4 (bottom/Rudie H. Kuiter), 5/bottom, 28/bottom (Norbert Rosing), 8 (top/J. A. L. Cooke), 12/top (John Paling), 14 (Mike Linley), 15, 16, 17/top (Michael Fogden), 17/bottom, 19/bottom (Zig Leszczynski), 20 (Babs and Bert Wells), 22 (both/Doug Allen), 29 (James D. Watt).

ROTHERHAM PUBLIC LIBRARIES

**This book must be returned by the date specified at the time of
issue as the Date Due for Return.**

**The loan may be extended (personally, by post or telephone) for
a further period, if the book is not required by another reader,
by quoting the above number**   **LM1 (C)**

Contents

Caring for the young

Most of the hundreds and thousands of different types of animals do not care for their young. Of the few that do look after their babies, many show only a very basic form of care, while for others, especially birds and mammals, a lot more care is needed to make sure they grow up to be adults.

◁ The short-horned female cricket cares for its young by drilling into the soil and laying her eggs with her ovipositor. By laying her eggs underground, she hides the eggs from enemies that would eat them.

◁ An animal can give its young a good chance of survival by protecting the eggs and young. The amazing-looking male seahorse has a pouch in which the eggs are placed. The eggs take four to five weeks to develop inside the cosy pouch. When they hatch, the baby seahorses look just like tiny copies of their parents.

Birds usually build nests and take great care of the eggs and chicks when they hatch. This common tern chick is begging for food from its parent. ▷

△ Cheetah cubs spend the first part of their life developing inside the protection of the mother's body. When they are born they feed on milk from their mother.

Mini-beasts

Some mini-beasts are very careful with their young. They bring them food and spend a lot of time looking after them.

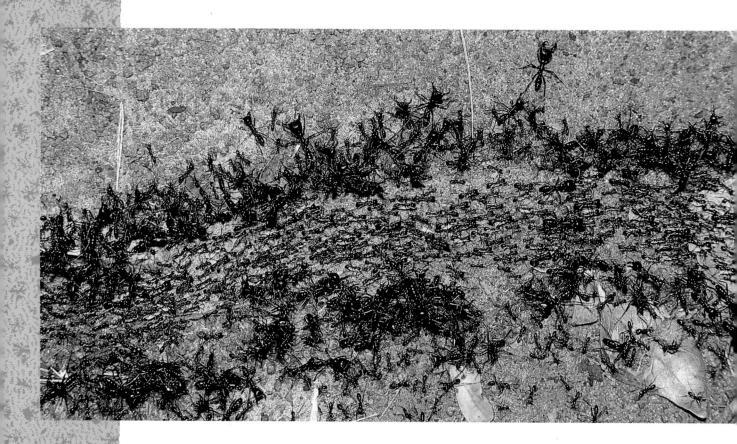

△ Ants live in societies with a queen, workers and males. Some also have soldiers which have large heads and strong jaws. This picture shows African driver worker ants carrying larvae while the soldiers stand guard. These ants do not have permanent nests, but set up camps before moving on, carrying their developing grubs with them.

△ Honeybee grubs are taken care of by worker bees. A queen bee lays an egg in each cell and the worker bees feed the growing grubs with honey.

Eventually, the young adult bees emerge from their cells. ▷
Their first duty will be to nurse the next generation of developing honeybees.

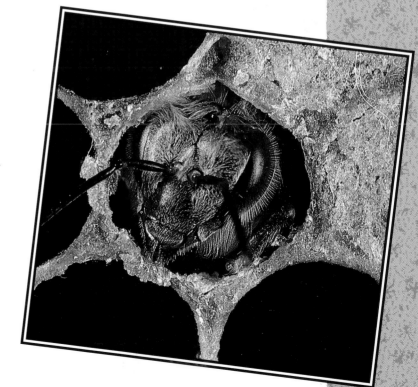

△ Many solitary insects – ones that live alone rather than in huge societies, like honeybees and ants – can be seen taking care of their young. A shield bug tends her family. She will sit over them to protect them from enemies.

◁ A sand wasp drags a large cricket to her burrow. Solitary wasps capture other mini-beasts and then paralyse them with their sting. The victims are still alive but cannot move when they are taken to the wasps' nests. Eggs are laid on the bodies of the mini-beasts and when the eggs hatch, the grubs have plenty of food to eat.

△ An ichneumon wasp uses her extremely long ovipositor to drill through wood to reach a hidden grub of another insect. Having found her victim, she will lay an egg on it. When the wasp's grub hatches, it will feed on its host.

Fish

Most fish do not care for their young. They simply release their eggs and sperm into the water and leave them to survive on their own. A large number of the baby fish die, so vast numbers of eggs are laid to ensure that at least some of them survive to adulthood. However, there are a number of exceptions to this rule.

△ The brightly-coloured male three-spined stickleback is a good father. Here he is making a nest from pieces of water plants which he sticks together with a sticky substance produced by his body.

◁ The female stickleback lays her eggs in the nest, then the male fertilizes them.

He guards the nest and also fans it with his fins so that the eggs are supplied with a stream of fresh water. ▷

He will look after the newly-hatched baby fish for about two weeks. ▷

◁ A female trout is about to lay her eggs. The larger male will quickly move in to fertilize them. They will leave the eggs alone and the baby fish that hatch must look after themselves.

△ The African mouthbrooder spits out a mouthful of tiny babies. She took the eggs into her mouth as soon as they were laid and they remained there until the young hatched. The baby fish will dash back into her mouth if danger threatens.

△ Some fish give birth to live young.
The female does not shed her eggs –
instead the baby fish develop inside her
body. When the time is right, the
Mexican swordtail jerks her body and
out pops a tiny fish.

Frogs, toads and salamanders

Most frogs and toads leave their eggs in ponds and show no interest in the tadpoles that hatch. But there are some who show great interest in the survival of their young and, like fish, the male may play a key role.

The female Costa Rican glass frog lays her eggs on a leaf above a stream. The male guards them for several days. When the tadpoles hatch, they wriggle down the leaf and fall into the water. ▽

◁ The European male midwife toad gathers the string of eggs laid by the female and wraps it round his back legs. He carries the eggs around for several weeks until they are ready to hatch. Then he lets the string go into the water.

The female poison dart frog carries two tadpoles on her back. She hops around the forest floor until she finds a plant with a pool of water at its base and then releases the tadpoles into the safety of the water. ▽

△ The babies of this marsupial frog developed inside the pouches on the mother's back. Now they are coming out.

△ Like frogs and toads, salamanders are amphibians, which means they can live both on the land and in the water. The marbled salamander guards its eggs. When the autumn rains flood the area, the eggs will hatch.

Reptiles

As a rule, reptiles are not good parents. The female lays the eggs and then she leaves them. Female green turtles bury their eggs on a tropical beach and then return to the sea. The newly-hatched young must try to reach the safety of the sea without the protection of a parent. ▷

◁ Crocodiles and alligators are very good parents. After these Nile crocodile eggs hatch, the young, which are fully formed and equipped with sharp teeth, stay with their huge mother for a short time.

Pythons will brood their large clutches of eggs. The female circles around the eggs until they hatch. Some snakes keep their eggs inside them, their bodies acting like a living nest, until the eggs are ready to hatch. ▷

The five-lined skink guarding its eggs that have started to hatch. Many skinks do not lay eggs but give birth to live young. ▽

Birds

Most birds take great care of their young. The eggs are usually incubated in the nest by one or both parents and the chicks are fed, protected and kept clean and warm by the adult birds.

△ Amazingly, the Australian mallee fowl incubates its eggs in a huge compost heap that it builds. The mallee fowl checks the nest's temperature continually, and if the compost gets too hot, it opens the nest to let out the heat.

△ An emperor goose
defends its clutch of
eggs from an intruder.
Throughout incubation,
the eggs are turned at
intervals so they are
warmed evenly.

◁ The male emperor penguin balances a single egg on his feet. He stands on the ice without feeding for up to two months while the female goes off to feed in the sea. A fold of skin covers the egg and protects it from the cold Antarctic winds.

A two-week-old emperor penguin chick rests on the feet of its parent. The mother returns when the chick is ready to hatch, her crop filled with fish for the chick. Now the male can return to the sea at last to catch something to eat. ▽

Baby birds need feeding until they leave the nest. This is a full-time job for the parents. A peregrine falcon feeding its chick. ▷

For safety, the chicks of birds that leave the nest soon after hatching, such as these mallard ducklings, must not become separated from their parent. As soon as they see their mother after hatching, they will follow her wherever she goes. The way they learn to know their parent is called imprinting. ▽

Mammals

Like birds, mammals take good care of their babies. The female feeds her young on milk, so she is often left to raise a family by herself.

△ A house mouse suckles her young. When they were born, she licked the blind, helpless babies clean, making sure the noses and mouths were free for breathing. If one strays from the nest, she will carry it back to safety.

A female red kangaroo does not build a nest because her baby is sheltered in her pouch. When the tiny baby is born, it crawls up through its mother's fur until it reaches the pouch. There it grasps a teat with its mouth and grows quickly, feeding on the milk. ▷

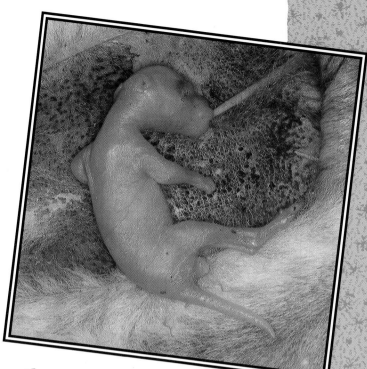

After about two months, the kangaroo joey will venture out of the pouch in search of food. After about nine months, it will be big enough to leave the pouch altogether and go off on its own. ▽

△ A wildebeest calf can follow its mother when it is only ten minutes old, and can run as fast as her within twenty-four hours. Living in the open country of Africa, if the calves could not keep up with their mothers, they would probably be eaten by a lion.

△ A grey seal pup suckling. The changeover from a diet of mother's milk to solid food is gradual for many mammals. But the grey seal mother will abandon its pup three weeks after birth. Then the pup has to feed and look after itself.

Baboons live on the ground and run on all fours, so the babies cling to their mothers' fur when moving from place to place. As they grow older, the babies stray further and further from the mothers, returning when frightened or hungry. ▷

◁ Meerkats live in groups in burrows. The young are often left by their mothers in the care of 'baby-sitters', other meerkats which take care of the young and keep a watchful eye out for danger.

A humpback whale calf swims close to its mother. The bond between them is very strong, and the mother must teach her calf many things, such as how to surface correctly in order to breathe. ▽

◁ Mammals often learn how to find or catch food by watching their mothers. At first the mother cheetah feeds her cubs on her milk. As the cubs grow, she will return from a hunt with meat for them to eat. Later, she will train them to kill live prey for themselves. Here she has returned with a young impala for them to kill.

Glossary

Brood To sit on or hatch eggs.

Burrow A hole or passage in the ground dug by an animal.

Cell A small compartment or 'room' that makes up the nests of bees and wasps.

Clutch A group of eggs laid by a bird.

Crop A pouch-like part of a bird's throat in which food is stored.

Fertilize To bring together a female egg and male sperm so that an animal will produce young.

Generation The next group of developing insects.

Host An animal that supports another animal.

Incubated Eggs that have been kept warm by an animal sitting on them.

Insects Small, six-legged creatures with a body separated into three parts.

Larvae Insects in the first stage of development after coming out of the egg. Also known as grubs.

Mammals Animals whose females give birth to live young which they feed with milk from their bodies.

Offspring The young of animals.

Ovipositor A part of most female insects for laying eggs.

Pouch A kind of pocket for carrying young.

Societies Groups of insects living together.

Spawning Laying eggs.

Sperm The fluid from a male that fertilizes the female egg.

Suckling Sucking milk from the teat of a mammal.

Survival Remaining alive.

Teat The part of a mammal through which milk passes to its young.

Books to read

Making a Nest, Paul Bennett (Wayland, 1994)
Changing Shape, Paul Bennett (Wayland, 1994)
Reproduction to Birth, Clint Twist (Watts, 1991)

How Nature Works, Steve Parker (Kingfisher, 1991)
Observing Nature series (Wayland): look for titles on ants, blackbirds, butterflies and frogs.

Notes for parents and teachers

Project: **Garden Wildlife**

Some animals spend a great deal of their time rearing and caring for their offspring. In other animals, the responsibility for their offspring ends when the eggs are laid. You may find examples of both of these types of animals in and around where you live. Nesting birds are interesting to watch. They may build a nest in a tree or hedge. You can try to encourage birds to nest in your garden by putting up a nest box. You may even see them collecting nesting materials. Observe the adult birds collecting food for their young, but do not approach the nest. Make a note of everything that you see.

You may also see other animals raising a family. Spiders lay their eggs in a protective cocoon. The female spiders of some species will guard the cocoon. If you have hedgehogs, foxes or badgers living near you, they may visit your garden for food and also bring along their offspring. If you have a pond, frogs may visit and lay their eggs. Frogs do not look after their young at all. Have a good look around your garden and see what you can find. If you do not have a garden, then visit a local park. Write all your observations in your nature diary.

Project: **Pets**

If you or a friend have any pets, you may have the opportunity to observe how they care for their young. Cats, dogs, rabbits and mice are all mammals and so the young stay with the adults until they are able to fend for themselves. The mother feeds her young on milk that she produces in her body.

If you have pet fish, frogs, reptiles or insects, they too may produce young. Observe them to see if the adults look after their young. Write any observations in your wildlife diary. Always remember not to disturb a mother with her young, even if they are pets.

Places to visit

You may see some of the animals mentioned in this book in a well run zoo or wildlife park.

Index

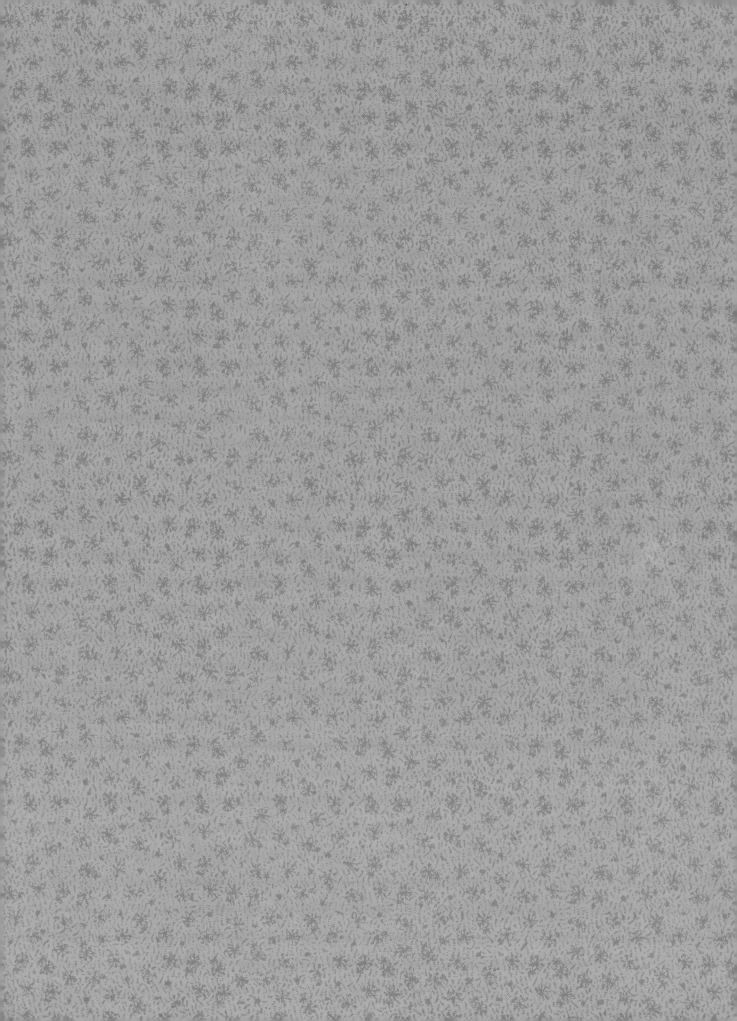